Advancing Reading Instruction

LEVEL 1A

♭ Piper Books

Instructions

- Remind the reader to 'Say the sounds' - not the letter-names
- Insist on accurate reading at all times
- Ensure attention is paid to word endings
- Avoid temptation to overhelp
- Never allow a guessing habit to develop
- Encourage rereading of earlier books with increased expression
- Use the stories and questions to develop speech, language and vocabulary
- On completion of each story, if using the Optional Questions encourage the learner to answer in full sentences and to reread the relevant page(s) if necessary

Linguistic Focus

ARI Level 1 introduces two-syllable words, reinforces vocabulary from BRI (Beginning Reading Instruction) Levels 1-3, and gradually introduces new letter-sound correspondences and suffixes. Over 400 new words lay the decoding foundations for a vastly expanded lexicon.

See › www.piperbooks.co.uk › RESOURCES › ARI free resources for ARI Level 1 Initial and Mastery Assessments and a book-by-book Pupil Progress Sheet, including a record of word, sound and letter(s) introduction and a tutor comments column.

Contents

Story 1: **Pan and the Pond** 5

Story 2: **The Box Trick**.....................13

Story 3: **Jack Gets Stuck** 23

Story 4: **Wink Naps** 33

Story 5: **The Trunk in the Well** 41

Story 6: **Lil Helps Tom** 51

Story 7: **The Shell**.........................59

Story 8: **Thanks to Bess** 69

Story 9: **The Ducks Go Camping** 77

Story 10: **The King's Ring**..................87

Story 11: **The Long Song**....................95

Story 12: **The King's Pond** 105

Story 13: **The Box Cave** 113

Story 14: **The Wisher**.......................121

STORY 1

Pan and the Pond

Story 1

Introducing:

Letter(s)	**Sound**	**Example**
(Grapheme)	(Phoneme)	
'ey'	/ae/	th<u>ey</u>

Contractions e.g. *can't, I'm, I'll*
Suffix 'ing' e.g. *going, playing*

Optional Questions

p8
Why can't Pat play with Pan?

p8-9
What is Pan's first idea for getting Pat across the pond?

p9
Why does Pat refuse to cross the pond?

p9-11
How do Dan and Pan solve the problem of getting Pat across the pond?

Pan and the Pond

Pan is playing in the pond. She sees Pat. She wants to play with him.

"Will you play with me?" yells Pan. "We can play on this rock."

"I want to play with you but I can't get there. I can't swim. I will sink in the pond," yells Pat.

"I'll help you," yells Pan. Pan has a sack. She picks it up. She runs up the hill.

Pan bends down to get rocks. She puts the rocks in her sack. She runs back to the pond.

Pan puts the rocks in the pond.

"Jump on the rocks, Pat," yells Pan.

"I can't jump there. I'll slip," yells Pat. "I'll sink in the pond."

"Dan is on the hill," yells Pan. "I'll ask him to help us.

"I need to cut a log," Pan said to Dan. "Will you help me?"

"Yes. I'm going to cut this tree. Then we'll cut a log," said Dan.

Dan and Pan cut the tree. The tree slams down. They bend down and cut a log. They roll it to the pond.

Now Pat can get there. He jumps on the log. He runs to Pan.

"Now we can play," yells Pan.

Pat is playing with Pan on the log on the pond. Dan is going back up the hill. He will cut down trees.

Story 2

The Box Trick

Story 2

No new letter-sound correspondences introduced.

Optional Questions

p16
What does Tom decide to do to Buck?

p18-19
Why does Bess collect a sack full of rocks?

p19
Why does Tom let Buck go?

What do you think of Tom's behaviour?

The Box Trick

This is Tom. He sits next to his den.

Buck and Bess are playing. They are playing next to the den. Tom sees them playing.

"I'll trick Buck," said Tom. "I'll put him in a box."

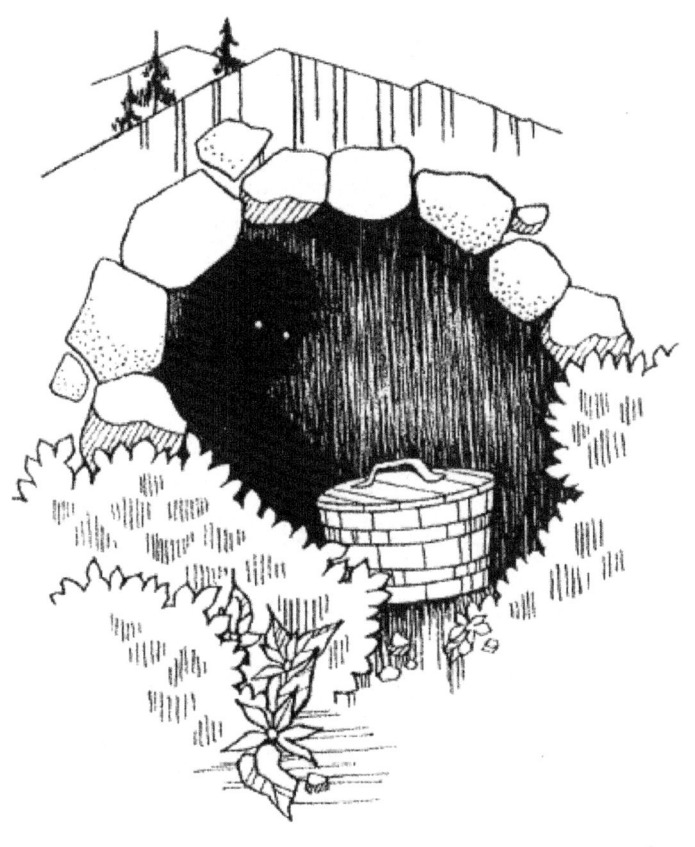

Tom gets a box. He tricks Buck and puts him in the box. Then Tom runs to the den. Buck is yelling. Tom puts a lid on the box.

Bess stops playing. She can see the den and the box. She can not see Buck.

"Buck must be in there. I'll yell to him," said Bess. "Buck, are you in there?" Bess yells.

She cannot see him. "Tom is playing a trick," said Bess. "Tom is in the den. Buck must be in the den, also. He must be in the box. I'll help Buck. I'll help him get out. I'll trick Tom."

Bess puts rocks in a sack. She runs to the den with the sack.

"I need a box with a lid," she yells to Tom. "I want to put this ham in the box."

Tom wants to put the ham in the box. Tom said, "I'll let Buck go." Tom, who is next to a tree, puts the box down. He lets Buck go.

Tom wants to trick Bess. He wants Bess to put the ham in the box. But Bess and Buck put the sack of rocks in the box. They want to trick Tom.

He thinks the box has the ham and he's going back to his den. "I'll keep this ham," Tom yells to them.

Bess and Buck run. They are going down the hill.

"It's fun to trick Tom," said Bess.

"But it's not fun to be put in Tom's box!" said Buck.

"No, no, that's not fun," adds Bess.

STORY 3

Jack Gets Stuck

Story 3

No new letter-sound correspondences introduced.

Optional Questions

p26
How do the three children hide?

p28
Why doesn't Jack get out of the bin?

p29
Who comes up with the plan to get Jack out of the bin?

Who do you think has the best hiding-place, and who has the worst?

Jack Gets Stuck

"Let's go out and play," said Kim to Jack. "We can ask Jill and Russ to play with us."

"Yes, let's go," said Jack.

Kim and Jack go out. They spot Jill and Russ. "There they are," said Jack.

"Will you play with us?" yells Kim.

"Yes, we'll play. I'll be it," said Jill.

Jill stands next to a tree trunk. "1, 2, 3, 4, 5..." she yells.

Kim jumps to the back of a tree. Russ runs and sits next to a box. Jack picks the cut grass out of a bin and jumps in.

"...8, 9, 10!" Jill stops.

Then she spots Kim. "Kim, I see you at the back of that tree trunk," she yells.

Jill spots Russ. "Russ, I see you," she said. "But I can't see Jack!"

Russ and Kim help Jill. "Jack is not on this log," said Kim. "He's not next to this tree trunk."

Then Jill said, "The grass is out of the bin. I think he's in there."

"Jack, I think you are in there," Jill said.

"Yes, I am," said Jack. "Now I want to get out." Then Jack yells, "I can't get out! I think I'm stuck."

Kim, Russ, and Jill help Jack but Jack is still stuck. "I'll run in and get Mum and Dad," said Kim. "They will help to lift you out."

"Can you help Jack?" Kim yells to Mum and Dad. "He hid in a bin and now he's stuck."

Mum and Dad go out to help. They lift Jack out of the bin.

"Now you must get all the grass and put it back in the bin," said Dad.

"And," said Mum, "you must not play in that bin."

"I will not play there," said Jack. "I am glad to be out."

STORY 4

Wink Naps

Story 4

No new letter-sound correspondences introduced.

Optional Questions

p35-36
Name five things that Wink does.

p37
Why are the fish worried about Wink?

p39
Why does the shell let Wink go?

p40
Why does Wink prefer the tug to the shell?

Wink Naps

Wink wants to play her drums. She is getting them out. She puts them next to a tug.

Then she sits on a trunk next to the tug. She is sitting there and now she is playing the drums.

"This is fun," said Wink.

Then Wink wants to nap. She spots a big shell. "I want to rest in this shell," said Wink. "I'll rest here."

Wink is getting in the shell. She puts her sack in the shell.

Six fish swim up to Wink.

Wink is resting in the shell. The shell will snap shut. This is bad. Wink will get shut in the shell! Now ten fish swim up to the shell.

Wink sees the shell snap shut. "This is a bad spot to be napping. I must get out of here," she thinks.

The shell is shut and Wink is still sitting in it. Wink thinks and thinks. She picks up her sack. She digs down in the sack and gets a pin. Wink thinks the pin will help her get out of the shell.

Wink sticks the shell with the pin.
"Stop! Stop sticking me," said the shell.

"Let me out and I'll stop," said Wink.

"Just stop sticking me with the pin. I'll let you go," said the shell.

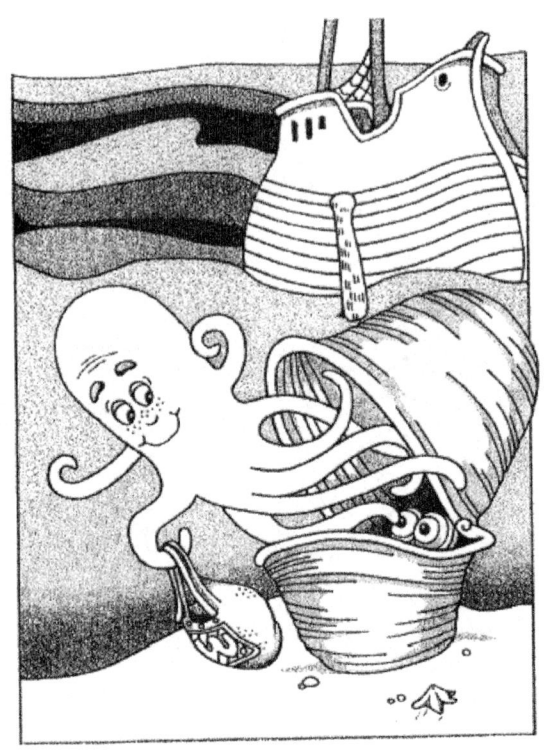

The lid of the shell lifts up and Wink jumps out. Then she runs to the tug. "I'll rest on that tug," said Wink.

Wink stands on the tug. She can't get stuck there.

STORY 5

The Trunk in the Well

Story 5

Introducing:

Letter(s) (Grapheme)	**Sound** (Phoneme)	**Example**
'y'	/ie/	m<u>y</u>

Optional Questions

p43
What is Lil collecting?

p44
Why does Lil tie a belt to her trunk?

p47
Why do Meg and Pat put the trunk down the well?

p49
Who opens the trunk – and how does she do it?

The Trunk in the Well

Lil is getting rocks from the pit.
She's putting the rocks in her trunk.

"There are ten rocks in my trunk.
I'll lock them up," said Lil. She puts
a lock on the trunk.

"Now I must get my trunk down
this hill," said Lil.

"I'll put this belt on my trunk. The belt will help me get the trunk down the hill. Then I'll put the trunk on my back," said Lil.

Lil is going down the hill. She is slipping. The belt is slipping.

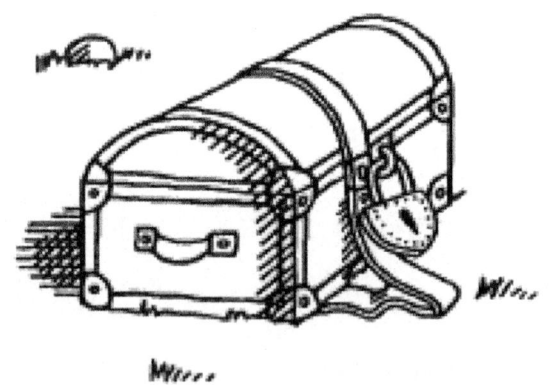

Lil stops by a well. "I want to go down the hill but I must stop. My trunk is slipping. I need to rest," said Lil. "A rest and a nap are all I need. I'll rest next to this well."

Meg and Pat see Lil napping by the well. Then Meg sees the trunk.

"Lil has a trunk," Meg tells Pat. "I want to see in the trunk. Help me."

Pat and Meg get the trunk. Meg slams a rock down on the lock.

"I can't smash this lock!" she said. "We can't peep in the trunk. I'm sad."

Pat sees that Lil is getting up from her nap. "Meg! Lil is getting up," he said. "Lil must not see us with this trunk."

Meg and Pat are putting the trunk down the well. "Now Lil can't see us with the trunk," said Meg. "Her trunk has sunk in the well."

Lil gets up. She can't see her trunk. All she sees are Meg and Pat.

"Did you see a trunk with a belt on it?" asks Lil. "I need the trunk."

Lil is sad.

Meg and Pat do not want Lil to be sad. They will help her.

"It's all a trick, Lil. The trunk is sunk in the well," Meg said.

"Will you help me get it?" asks Lil. "There are ten rocks in my trunk. We can play with them."

"Yes, we'll help you," yell Meg and Pat. Meg and Pat help Lil get the trunk out of the well.

The trunk is still shut. Lil picks the lock with a pin.

"Now the lock is not on the trunk," Lil said. "We can all play with my rocks."

STORY 6

Lil Helps Tom

Story 6

Introducing:

Suffix 'ed' e.g. *wanted, asked, landed*

Optional Questions

p53
Why does Lil visit Tom?

p54
How is Lil feeling, and why?

p55
What happens to Tom?

p57-58
How does Lil manage to get Tom out of the mud?

Lil Helps Tom

Lil had a drum. She needed help getting up the hill.

"I think I'll go and ask Tom to help me," said Lil.

Tom had a den. It was on top of the hill. Lil went to the den.

"Will you help me? Help me get my drum up the hill," Lil said to Tom.

Tom just wanted to nap. He did not want to help Lil.

"Get out of my den. Let me nap," he yelled at Lil.

Lil went back down the hill. She sat down in the grass. She sat next to her drum.

"I'm sad," said Lil. "I need help with this drum."

Tom jumped up from his nap. "I want to go down to the pond," he said. "I think I'll go swimming."

Tom ran down the path. He fell. He landed in the mud pit next to Lil.

"I'm stuck and I can't get out. Help! Help! I'm not swimming, I'm sinking," Tom yelled to Lil.

"Am I needed?" asked Lil.

"Yes, I need you to help me get out," said Tom. "I landed in the mud. Now I'm stuck."

"I asked you to help me. I needed help with my drum but you wanted to nap," said Lil.

"Get me out. I'll help you with the drum," said Tom.

"Then I will help you," Lil said.

Lil needed help to get Tom out. She jumped up and landed on a rock by the mud pit. Then she jumped from the rock. She landed on top of her drum. She jumped up and down on the drum. The drum went Bam! Bam! Bam!

A man ran down the path. He had a stick with him.

"Did you play the drum? Am I needed?" asked the man.

"Yes," said Lil. "I wanted you to help get Tom out of the mud."

"This stick will help," said the man.

The man helped Tom out of the mud pit.

Tom said, "You helped me. Now I'll be glad to help Lil."

So Tom put Lil and the drum on his back. Then they went up the hill.

STORY 7

The Shell

Story 7

No new letter-sound correspondences introduced.

Optional Questions

p61
Name three different things the girls are doing, or planning to do, at the seaside.

p63
Why are Beth and Bob arguing?

p65
How do Bob and Beth lose their shell?

Who do you think is in the right?

The Shell

Jill and Beth are playing on the sand. Beth is picking up shells. She has a box to put them in. Jill is going to fish and swim.

Vic and Russ are on the bank. Vic and Russ sit and fish. Jill will fish with them.

Bob wants to pick up shells. He has a sack to put them in.

Bob sees a shell in the sand. He bends down to pick it up. Beth sees the shell. She bends down to pick it up but Bob gets it.

"I want that shell," yells Beth. "It's the best."

"No! No! I need it," yells Bob.

Beth yells at Bob and Bob yells back at Beth.

Jill asks Bob to stop yelling.

Russ wants them to stop. "Let Bob keep the shell," he yells to Beth.

"No! No! Let Beth keep it," they yell.

Vic stops fishing. He jumps from the bank. He runs to help.

"Let go of that shell," Vic yells at Bob.

Bob and Beth will not put the shell down.

Bob slips in the sand by the bank. Beth trips. The shell slips.

"Get it! Get it!" yells Beth. But the shell sinks in the sand.

Bob and Beth can't see it.

"There is a shell," yells Beth. She picks it up. "This is the best shell here." She puts it in the box. She puts it with all her shells.

Then Bob picks up a shell. "I think this is the best of all." He puts it in the sack with all his shells.

Vic, Jill and Russ go back to the bank to fish.

Bob and Beth keep picking up the shells. Bob thinks that he has the best shells but Beth thinks that she has the best shells of all.

STORY 8

Thanks to Bess

Story 8

No new letter-sound correspondences introduced.

Optional Questions

p71
How does Pam suggest they get up the hill?

p73
Why doesn't Pam see Buck go to the pond?

p74
Why does Buck fall into the pond?

Do you think Buck was reckless or just unlucky?

Thanks to Bess

Buck and Bess went out to play with Pam. Pam spotted grass on top of a hill.

"Let's go up there," she said. "We can skip up the hill and stop at the top."

The hill had trees and a lot of grass. Pam sat down on the hill next to a tree. She wanted to rest.

Buck and Bess stopped to play in the grass. "I want to skip in the grass," said Bess.

Buck and Bess played on the hill. Pam napped next to the tree.

Buck spotted a pond. He skipped down the hill to the pond. Pam still napped.

She did not see Buck go to the pond but Bess did.

Buck jumped and skipped on the rocks. He jumped from rock to rock. Then he landed on a wet rock. He fell in the pond!

Bess spotted Buck sinking in the pond. She stopped to think. "Buck can't swim! He will sink. Pam must help get Buck out of the pond."

Bess dashed back to the tree. Pam still napped. Bess wanted Pam to see Buck in the pond.

"I'm going to nip Pam. That will make her get up," said Bess.

Bess bent down and nipped Pam.

"Go and play, Bess," said Pam. But Bess nipped and nipped Pam.

"Bad Bess!" Pam yelled.

Then she spotted Buck sinking in the pond.

Pam ran. She dashed out on the rocks and helped Buck out of the pond.

"Thank you, Bess," said Pam. "You helped Buck a lot. He can't swim. He just sinks."

Story 9

The Ducks Go Camping

Story 9

Introducing:

Letter(s)	Sound	Example
(Grapheme)	(Phoneme)	
'ai'	/ae/	s<u>ai</u>l

Possessive nouns e.g. *Dan's, Meg's, man's*

Optional Questions

p79-80
Why are the ducks yelling for help?

p81
Why do the ducks refuse to go on the raft?

p83
How does the man feel about the ducks getting away?

What do you think of the man's behaviour?

The Ducks Go Camping

Meg has a raft. She sails her raft on the pond.

She sees Dan and Ann, the ducks, running down a hill to the pond. Dan has a tent. Ann has a trunk. Meg spots a man with a stick running behind the ducks.

"Help! Help!" yell the ducks. "We wanted to camp on the hill but we can't. This is the man's hill. He said we must go."

"I can help you," said Meg. "I can sail to you."

Meg's raft landed on the bank next to the ducks.

"Now just jump on this raft," yelled Meg.

"No, I can't," yelled Dan.

"I can't," yelled Ann.

"Yes, you can," said Meg. "Just jump!"

"We need the tent and the trunk," called the ducks.

Ann and Dan slid the tent and the trunk down to Meg. Meg put Dan's tent and Ann's trunk on the raft. Then Ann and Dan slid down the bank to the raft.

"We'll sail out on the pond," said Meg. "Then the man can't get us." Meg's raft sailed out on the pond.

The man dashed to the bank. He jumped up and down. Meg's raft did not stop.

This big man yelled and yelled. Meg's raft went on sailing and the big man just went on yelling.

Now Meg, Dan and Ann are sitting on Meg's raft. The raft is sailing on the pond.

"Let's land it next to the trees," said Ann.

"We can camp there," said Dan.

The ducks jumped to the bank. Meg helped put Dan's tent and Ann's trunk on the bank.

Meg helped the ducks put up the tent. Then she helped with the trunk.

"I will go now," she said.

"You must not go!" said the ducks. "All of us can camp here."

Meg and the ducks sat on Ann's trunk in Dan's tent. "This is not a bad spot to camp," they said, "not a bad spot at all."

STORY 10

The King's Ring

Story 10

Introducing:

Single-syllable, one phoneme 'ng' ending e.g. *ring, song, strong*

Optional Questions

p91
Why does Rex plan to steal the ring?

p92
How does Rex steal the ring?

p92-93
Name the three ways Rex tries to open the box.

p94
Why will Rex never be able to use the wishing ring?

The King's Ring

This is the king and he wants to wish. And so he gets his wishing ring out. This ring can bring him the wish he wants.

"Bring me the best ham in the land," said the king. The ring did what he said. "Ring, bring me this and bring me that." The ring did it all.

Rex sat next to his king. "This ring brings the king lots of things," said Rex. "I want the king's ring."

Rex sat there thinking and thinking. "I need things. I can get them with a wishing ring. The king will go to bed. Then I'll get the ring. I can get all the things I want."

The king locked the ring in a box and went to bed. The box had a strong lock on it.

"The king is resting now. I'll get the wishing ring," said Rex. He picked up the box. Then he dashed down the hill and hid in the trees.

"I must get the ring out of this box. The box is locked and the lock is strong. I must think," said Rex.

"A song! I can sing a song and get the ring out," he yelled.

The song did not get the ring out.

Rex jumped up and went to get a pin. He stuck the pin in the lock. He still did not get the ring out.

Next Rex spotted a rock. He smashed the lock with a rock. The strong lock did not crack!

"I still can't get the ring out of this box," yelled Rex. "I'll run back to the king. Then I can see the king get it out."

Rex put the box next to the king's bed. Then Rex hid.

The king jumped up from his bed. "Ring," said the king, "ask the box to let you out."

The ring jumped out of the box. Then the king put on the ring. He shut the box.

"A wish!" said Rex. "The king can get the ring out with a wish! It is the king's ring. Just the king can wish with the ring."

Story 11

The Long Song

Story 11

Introducing:

Letter(s) (Grapheme)	Sound (Phoneme)	Example
'ar'	/ar/	C<u>ar</u>los

Two-syllable names e.g. *Rosa, Anna, Carlos*

Optional Questions

p97
Who is going shopping, who is going to the bank, and who is supposed to be cutting the grass?

p99-101
How does Anna try to make Rosa mow the lawn? Does it work?

p101-103
How does Rosa try to make Anna mow the lawn? Does it work?

What do you think of Rosa's behaviour?

The Long Song

"Carlos and I are going shopping," said Dad.

"I need to go to the bank," said Mum. "I'll go with you."

"Rosa," said Dad, "I want you to cut the grass. It's getting long. Anna can help you cut it."

Then Mum, Carlos, and Dad went out.

Rosa sat down to play with a ball.

"Dad asked us to cut the grass," said Anna. "He'll be back and the grass will not be cut."

Rosa just sat there playing. She did not want to cut the grass. She wanted Anna to cut it.

Anna wanted Rosa to cut it.

"Tap, tap, tap," Rosa just tapped her ball.

Now Anna began to think. "I want Rosa to cut the grass. I'll trick her."

"Rosa," yelled Anna, "will you go out and get the mop?" Rosa went out to bring in the mop.

Then Anna locked Rosa and the mop out. "Now Rosa will cut the grass."

Rosa rang the bell. "Let me in," she yelled. Rosa rang and rang. Anna did not let her in.

"You are playing a bad trick on me," Rosa yelled.

Then Rosa stopped to think. "I'll trick Anna," she said. "I'll sing to her."

Rosa did not sing well but she sang a long, long song. "It's fun to cut the grass," she sang.

"Rosa is singing a song out there," said Anna. "She keeps singing that it is fun to cut the grass."

"Stop that singing," Anna yelled but Rosa went on singing.

"Cutting the grass is fun, fun, fun!" sang Rosa.

"Stop it. Stop it now," Anna went on.

"Cutting the grass is lots of fun!" sang Rosa.

Anna went out to Rosa. "Rosa, I want to sing. Let me help you cut the grass," said Anna.

Rosa just sang.

"I want to cut the grass with you," Anna yelled. "Let me! Let me!"

"Well," said Rosa, "I'll let you cut the grass." She stopped singing and sat down to play.

Anna did not see that Rosa had played a trick on her. She cut the grass. She sang a long, long song. Then Rosa said, "I think the grass is cut now. Thank you, Anna."

STORY 12

The King's Pond

Story 12

Introducing:

Letter(s) (Grapheme)	Sound (Phoneme)	Example
'a-e'*	/ae/	at<u>e</u>

split digraph

Optional Questions

p107
What does Hank use as a fishing rod?

p109

How and why does the King punish Hank?

p111
How does Hank escape?

p112
Do you agree that the fish should be for everybody?

106

The King's Pond

Big Hank went down to the king's pond to fish. He had a string with a pin on it. He put the string in the pond. It came up with a fish on it.

Big Hank ate the fish. Then he sat down to take a rest.

The king of the land came down the path. He spotted Hank's string and the pin. "Did you take a fish from this pond?" asked the king.

"Yes, I did," said Big Hank, "and I ate it."

"That is bad," said the king. "You can't fish in this pond. The fish are just for me. They are not for you."

"You ate a fish from the pond," said the king. "That was a bad thing. It was my fish. My big fish. For that I will lock you to this tree."

The king made Hank stand up. Then he locked him to the trunk of the tree.

"This is a strong lock," said the king.

"You can't snap it," he added.

Then he went down the path.

"I am strong," said Hank. "I can get out of this. I can snap the lock."

He hit the lock with a stick. Bang! The lock did not snap. He hit the lock with a rock. Bang! Bang! The lock still did not snap.

Just then a man with a stick came down the path. "Help me," said Hank. "The king locked me to this tree. I can't snap the lock."

The man gave his stick to Big Hank. "Take this stick," he said. "It is made for snapping locks and things. It has a spell on it. The spell will snap the lock."

Hank hit the lock with the stick. Bang! The lock snapped!

"Thank you for helping me," said Hank. Then he gave back the stick with a spell on it.

"You did not need to hit and bang the lock. This spell can snap a lock with just a tap," the man with the stick said.

"But I'm glad I helped," said the man. "The king will be mad. But he can't take all the fish. The fish in this pond are for all to take."

Story 13

The Box Cave

Story 13

Introducing:

Letter(s) (Grapheme)	**Sound** (Phoneme)	**Example**
'i-e'*	/ie/	t<u>i</u>m<u>e</u>

split digraph

Optional Questions

p115
Why do Beth and Bob want boxes?

p118
What are Vic's problems?

p118
How is Vic feeling - happy? Frightened? Hungry?

p119-120
How is Beth planning to help Vic? Does it work?

The Box Cave

Beth and Bob wanted to make a cave out of boxes. They went to a shop and asked for them. The man at the shop gave them all the boxes he had.

"Let's make a cave with ten paths," said Beth. "All the paths can be just the same."

"This will be fun," said Bob. "Let's go, go, go!"

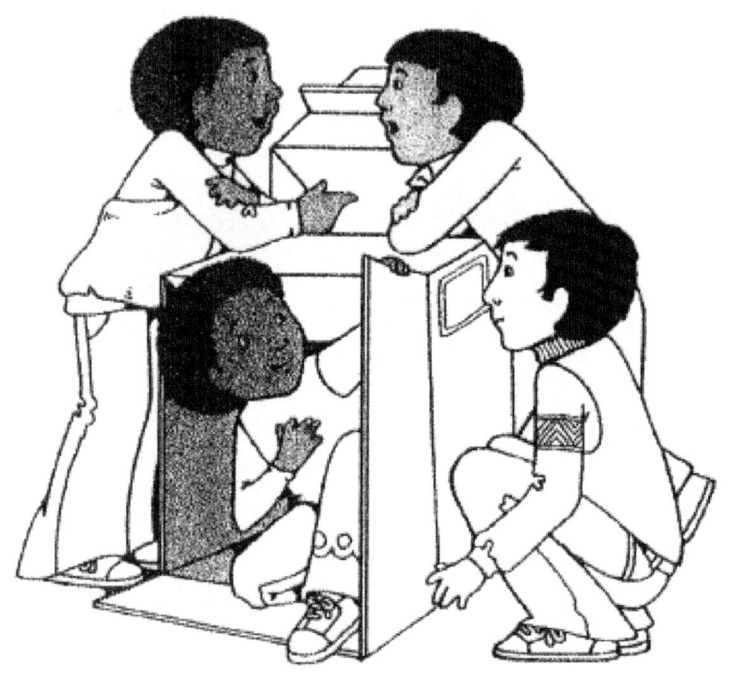

Beth and Bob set up all the boxes. They made a cave with ten paths. Then Vic and Carlos came to play with them.

"We can play a game in this cave," Beth said.

"Is this cave dark?" asked Vic.

"I think it will be," said Beth. "But it will be safe. We made it strong. Go in."

Vic went in the cave. "The cave is dark but this game is fun," he yelled from the cave. He was in the cave for a long, long time.

"I want to go in next," Bob yelled to Vic. "Time is running out. It's getting late. See the time."

"I can't see the time. It is dark in here. But you can get in now," Vic yelled back. "All the paths are the same. I think I'm in the last part of the cave. You can take the path at the start. That bit is not so dark."

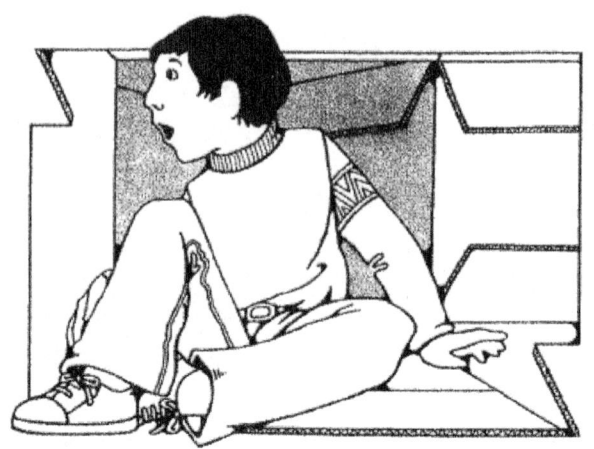

When Bob came out of the cave Vic was still in there.

"Vic has been there for a long time," said Carlos.

Carlos yelled, "Vic, get out of the cave. It's late and we must go now."

"I can't get out," yelled Vic. "All the boxes are long. All the paths are the same. It's dark. I'm in a trap. This game is not safe!"

"Vic is trapped in the dark boxes," said Beth. "I think I can help him out."

Beth picked up a stick. "I'll bang on top of the cave," she yelled to Vic. "That will help you take the best path."

Bang! Bang! Beth drummed on the ten boxes.

Vic went down a path to the left of the cave. Bang! Bang! The stick banged on top of the cave.

Bang! Bang! Beth hit the boxes hard.

"Keep it up," yelled Vic. "I think I'm on the path out of the cave."

Bang! Bang! Beth went on hitting the boxes. "Are you coming out, Vic?"

Then Vic came out of the cave.

"He's safe!" yelled Carlos.

"Thanks for helping me, Beth," said Vic.

Story 14

The Wisher

Story 14

No new letter-sound correspondences introduced.

Optional Questions

p123-124
Do you think Kate is mean or just sensible for not wanting to give away her fish?

p125
Do you think Kate is mean or just sensible for not wanting to share her fire?

p128
Should Dot have wished for something better than a ride?

Why does the Wisher call Dot 'kind'?

The Wisher

Dot and Kate set up camp next to a pond. Kate made a fire. She put fish in a pan on the fire.

Wanda the Wisher came out of the trees. "Let's hide the fish," said Kate, "Wanda the Wisher will take them from us."

"I will not hide mine," said Dot.

Then Wanda came up to the fire. "I see a fish," she said.

"You can't take this fish," said Kate. "It's mine."

But Dot gave Wanda the Wisher her fish. She ate it up.

"Thank you," said Wanda. Then she went to the pond for a swim.

"Wanda the Wisher will want to sit down at the fire," said Kate. "Let's put it out."

"No," said Dot. "We must ask her to sit with us. She is cold."

Then Wanda the Wisher came back from the pond. "I'm wet and cold," she said. "Let me sit next to the fire."

"This log is mine," said Kate. "You can't sit on it."

"Then sit with me, Wanda," said Dot.

The Wisher sat down.

"That is kind, Dot," she said. "I am cold but the fire is hot."

"It is getting late. It is time to rest," said the Wisher. "Will you let me go with you and rest in the tent?"

Kate wanted to stop her but Dot said, "Let the Wisher go in the tent. It is time for her to rest."

Wanda the Wisher lifted the flap of the tent and went in.

"Let's hide the drums," said Kate. "The Wisher will take them from us."

"No, we will not hide the drums," said Dot. "Wanda will not take them from us."

The Wisher came out of the tent.

"You must not hide drums from me, Kate," she said. "I am Wanda the Wisher!"

"I think you will take them from us," said Kate.

"No, no. I do not take things."

Then Wanda said, "Dot, you are kind. You gave me fish and a fire. You let me go in the tent. You did not hide things from me. Now you can ask me for a wish."

"I want to go on a ride with you," said Dot.

Wanda the Wisher and Dot went on a ride. Up, up they went.

When Wanda and Dot came back from the ride Dot said, "That was a big trip and a fast ride. Thank you, Wanda."

"I am sad," said Kate. "I did not get to ask for a wish. From this time on I will not hide things."

The big trip.

Stories in
ARI: Advanced Reading Instruction Programme:

ARI Level 1A – 14 Stories
ARI Level 1B – 14 Stories

ARI Level 2A – 21 Stories
ARI Level 2B – 20 Stories

ARI Level 3A – 19 Stories
ARI Level 3B – 19 Stories
ARI Level 3C – 18 Stories

This edition of ARI (Advanced Reading Instruction) Level 1A
Published in 2020 by Piper Books Ltd
United Kingdom

www.piperbooks.co.uk
enquiries@piperbooks.co.uk

This updated book was designed, formatted and produced by Piper Books Ltd

Optional Questions, updated text and illustrations © Piper Books Ltd

Printed in Great Britain
by Amazon